Dr. Livingstone,

I Presume

2018

By Dr. Delron Shirley
Cover Design By: Jeremy Shirley

Cover Image, Courtesy of:
Wellcome Collection.

Table of Contents

Dr. Livingstone, I Presume 5
Skin Color 6
Language 9
Eyes 17
Ears 23
Feet 32
Hands 37
Knees 39
Heart 43
Mouth 46
Conclusion 48
Teach All Nations Mission 49
Books by Delron & Peggy Shirley 51

This teaching manual is intended for personal study; however, the author encourages all students to also become teachers and to share the truths from this text with others. However, copying the text itself without permission from the author is considered plagiarism, which is punishable by law. To obtain permission to quote material from this book, please contact:

Delron Shirley
3210 Cathedral Spires Dr.
Colorado Springs, CO 80904
www.teachallnationsmission.com
teachallnations@msn.com

Dr. Livingstone, I Presume

Probably the most famous quote in all the annals of missionary history is the greeting of newsman and adventurer Henry Stanley when he finally reached missionary and explorer David Livingstone in the remote interior of Africa, "Dr. Livingstone, I presume?" On this encounter of November 10, 1871, there was really no reason for Stanley to make any other assumption than that this lone white man in the sea of black faces in the inner reaches of this hitherto-unexplored region of the world would be none other than Scottish missionary – David Livingstone.

When the term "missionary" is mentioned, some people immediately get a vision of a tall white colonial figure in a pith helmet carrying a big black Bible, marching through the jungle, attacking venomous snakes with one blow of his machete. Others imagine an elderly, humorless spinster with an accordion teaching little black children to sing "Jesus loves me."

But in this little study, I'd like to consider how we can really pick out who is a missionary. With Livingstone and the hypothetical missionaries in the previous paragraph, the dead-give-away clue was the skin color, but I'd like to suggest that the pigment in the skin isn't the real determining factor because they don't change. If a man is white, black, or orange polka-dotted before he is born again, he'll still be white, black, or orange polka-dotted after conversion – and he'll still be white, black, or orange polka-dotted if he is called into mission work. But there are some characteristic indicators that do go through radical changes when an individual is commissioned into this great ministry – distinctive gauges that uniquely identify him or her as a real "Dr. Livingstone."

Skin Color

It goes without saying that missionaries who come from other cultures to work among people of a different background and ethnic origin are going to "stick out like a sore thumb" because of their skin color. In my travels around the world, I've been seriously aware of the fact that my white face drew a lot of attention. Once in a remote area of India – so remote that the women wore no clothing above the waist – I had to become accustomed to having the people on the street stop whatever they were doing just to stare at me since they had never seen a man without a nice brown tone to his skin. In the hinterlands of the Himalayas, the children sometimes ask my wife if they could touch her since they weren't exactly sure if her pale skin would be the same as theirs. And, of course, I have published dozens of newsletters of our mission work in Africa with photos of black congregations and one lone white face notably shining out.

But there is one humorous story that I'd like to share. When the stewardess on a flight into Nigeria came through the cabin to distribute the landing forms, she had to confirm who was a citizen of Nigeria in order to make sure that she handed them the correct form. When she came to me, she asked, "Are you a Nigerian?" As I reached out to collect the paper, I held my hand close enough to her face that she couldn't mistake my skin color and answered that I was an American. When I arrived in Lagos, I told the story to my host and added that I was imagining that the love that I have for Africa on the inside had actually begun to show on the outside.

Speaking of Nigeria, let me share with you the story of the woman who brought the gospel to that nation when it was known as Calabar – Mary Slessor (1848 – 1915). She had an African heart housed inside a European body – so much so that she became known as "The White Queen of

Calaba" and "The White Queen of the Cannibals." Born in Scotland, Mary grew up in slums with an alcoholic father who only worked part of the time. When the father died, Mary was forced to go to work in the factory at the age of fourteen to support her family. Her mother was a devout Christian and very interested in the missionary movement of the time – an interest that she passed on to her daughter. After reading of the explorations of David Livingstone, Mary decided to dedicate her life to missions as well. At the age of twenty-eight, she sailed for Calabar to work among the tribal peoples who practiced many primitive customs such as wholesale human sacrifice of tribe members at the death of the chief since it was believed that the tribal leader needed an entourage of subjects to accompany him into the afterlife. Mary was especially moved by the custom of infanticide of twins because of a belief that one of the twins was a demon. Since they had no way of knowing which was the devil's child, both had to be destroyed. She took it upon herself to adopt every child she found abandoned – saving hundreds of twins by sending out other missioners to find, protect, and care for them. She also helped to put an end to a practice of determining guilt by making the suspects drink poison.

    Reasoning that her teachings and the fact that she was a woman would be less threatening to unreached tribes, Mary established herself in an area where previous male missionaries had been killed – and she was able to stay there for fifteen years, focusing on evangelism, settling disputes, encouraging trade, establishing social changes, and introducing Western education. Because of her outstanding success, she was actually appointed to a government position – vice-consul over the native court. Eventually, she was named vice-president of the local native court.

Even though she often suffered from malaria, she never gave up her mission work to return to Scotland – even when she had to be pushed around in a hand-cart because she could no longer walk. She might have been European on the outside, but she was definitely African on the inside because it was really Jesus inside of her!

I remember a movie that I saw as a very young child about Henry Stanley's quest for Dr. Livingstone. As he followed one dead-end lead after another, he was really encouraged when someone unquestionably confirmed that there was a white man living in a village in a distant area. After a long and tiring trek, he finally came to the village – only to discover that the man was an albino rather than a European. I have no idea if the scene was based on any historical truth, but it does make the point that there is something about a true man or woman of God that is unique and distinct. Even though there may be some who may seem to have the outward appearance, the "real McCoy" will eventually be evident. "Can the Ethiopian change his skin, or the leopard his spots? then may ye also do good, that are accustomed to do evil." (Jeremiah 13:23)

This is just one more confirmation of the truth that the prophet Samuel learned on the day that God directed him to anoint David rather than one of his tall, handsome, muscular older brothers, "The Lord seeth not as man seeth; for man looketh on the outward appearance, but the Lord looketh on the heart." (I Samuel 16:7)

Language

Missionaries, of course, speak a different language from the culture that they are ministering to. One of the major hurdles that they must cross is becoming conversant in the language of the people that they intend to reach. Even more importantly, they must understand the minor nuances of that language in order to properly communicate the gospel fluently. One interesting example of this principle occurred when the New Testament was translated into the language of an unreached people group. Since the language was previously not recorded, the translators had to start by developing a vocabulary, systemizing the grammar, and essentially making a dictionary of their words. Once the New Testament was translated, the missionaries thought that the people would respond to the gospel message; however, no one seemed interested. More than a decade later, the missionaries understood that they had mistranslated one significant word – sin. They had used a word that meant to get caught. As they became more familiar with the language, they discovered another word that actually conveyed the message of wrongdoing. Once they rewrote the Bible with this new word, the people began to accept the gospel since it now was the answer to their wrongdoings, not just the fact that they got caught.

However, the lesson that I want to communicate here is that missionaries also speak a different language from average Christians. Their speech is filled with the positive, aggressive words of advancement of the gospel – not the mediocre status-quo vocabulary of so many church members. I heard one great example when a missionary friend was relating his experiences behind the Iron Curtain before the fall of the Berlin Wall and his further ventures into radical Islam regions. After telling about having been taken hostage and a gun being held to his head, he concluded with, "Or you can just stay home and watch TV!"

Let me share some quotes from the mouth of one of the great missionaries who truly had the vocabulary of a world changer – Hudson Taylor (1832 – 3 June 1905).

James Hudson Taylor, known as the Father of Faith Missions, was founder of the China Inland Mission. He spent more than fifty years in China, living by faith – without the support of a sending agency. The society that he began was responsible for bringing over eight hundred missionaries to the country who began one hundred twenty-five schools and directly resulted in eighteen thousand Christian conversions, as well as the establishment of more than three hundred stations of work with more than five hundred local helpers in all eighteen provinces of China. Hudson Taylor was known for his sensitivity to Chinese culture and zeal for evangelism. He adopted the native Chinese clothing – a practice that actually brought ridicule from the other missionaries in China. He was especially notable for his determination to reach all of China, not just the coastal cities where most other missionaries congregated because of the safety in these colonized areas. Undeterred by any hardships he would endure, Hudson Taylor buried two wives and five children in China's soil but kept on with his work.

As a child of only five years, Hudson Taylor decided, *When I am a man, I mean to be a missionary and go to China.*

As a young man, he declared, *I feel I cannot go on living unless I do something for China.*

As an old man, he wrote, *If I had a thousand lives, I'd give them all for China.*

I am no longer anxious about anything, as I realize the Lord is able to carry out His will, and His will is mine. It makes no matter where He places me, or how. That is rather for Him to consider than for me; for in the easiest positions He must give me His grace, and in the most difficult, His grace is sufficient.

When I cannot read, when I cannot think, when I cannot even pray, I can trust.

Do not have your concert first, and then tune your instrument afterwards. Begin the day with the Word of God and prayer, and get first of all into harmony with Him.

All God's giants have been weak men who did great things for God because they reckoned on God being with them.

There are three stages to every great work of God: first it is impossible, then it is difficult, then it is done.

It does not matter how great the pressure is. What really matters is where the pressure lies – whether it comes between you and God, or whether it presses you nearer His heart.

Depend on it. God's work done in God's way will never lack God's supply. He is too wise a God to frustrate His purposes for lack of funds, and He can just as easily supply them ahead of time as afterwards, and He much prefers doing so.

It is not so much the greatness of our troubles, as the littleness of our spirit, which makes us complain.

The Great Commission is not an option to be considered; it is a command to be obeyed.

If I had a thousand pounds, China should have it. If I had a thousand lives, China should have them. No! Not China, but Christ. Can we do too much for Him? Can we do enough for such a precious Savior?

God isn't looking for people of great faith, but for individuals ready to follow Him.

Not by discussions nor by argument, but by lifting up Christ shall we draw men unto Him.

God uses men who are weak and feeble enough to

lean on him.

it is no small comfort to me to know that God has called me to my work, putting me where I am and as I am. I have not sought the position, and I dare not leave it. He knows why He places me here – whether to do, or learn, or suffer.

God wants you to have something far better than riches and gold, and that is helpless dependence upon Him.

To me it seemed that the teaching of God's Word was unmistakably clear: "Owe no man anything." To borrow money implied to my mind a contradiction of Scripture – a confession that God had withheld some good thing, and determination to get for ourselves what He had not given.

Let us give up our work, our thoughts, our plans, ourselves, our lives, our loved ones, our influence, our all, right into His hand, and then, when we have given all over to Him, there will be nothing left for us to be troubled about, or to make trouble about.

Jesus is our strength, and what we cannot do or bear, He can both do and bear in us.

The real secret of an unsatisfied life lies too often in an unsurrendered will.

O Lord, how happy should we be If we would cast our care on Thee. If we from self would rest, and feel at heart that One above. In perfect wisdom, perfect love Is working for the best!

I am more than ever convinced that if we were to take the directions of our Master and the assurances He gave to His first disciples more fully as our guide, we should find them to be just as suited to our times as to those in which they were originally given.

We have, then, in this beautiful section, as we have seen, a picture of unbroken communion and its delightful issues. May our lives correspond! First, one with the King, then speaking of the King; the joy of communion leading to fellowship in service, to a being all for Jesus, ready for any experience that will fit for further service, surrendering all to Him, and willing to minister all for Him. There is no room for love of the world here, for union with Christ has filled the heart; there is nothing for the gratification of the world, for all has been sealed and is kept for the Master's use. Jesus, my life is Thine! And evermore shall be hidden in Thee. For nothing can untwine Thy life from mine.

She would fain claim him fully, without giving up herself fully to him; but it can never be: while she retains her own name, she can never claim his. She may not promise to love and honor if she will not also promise to obey: and till her love reaches that point of surrender she must remain an unsatisfied lover – she cannot, as a satisfied bride, find rest in the home of her husband. While she retains her own will, and the control of her own possessions, she must be content to live on her own resources; she cannot claim his. Separation never comes from His side. He is always ready for communion with a prepared heart, and in this happy communion the bride becomes ever fairer, and more like to her Lord. She is being progressively changed into His image, from one degree of glory to another, through the wondrous working of the Holy Spirit, until the Bridegroom can declare, "Thou art all fair, My love; And there is no spot on thee." And now she is fit for service, and to it the Bridegroom woos her; she will not now misrepresent Him.

I believe we are all in danger of accumulating – it may be from thoughtlessness, or from pressure of occupation – things which would be useful to others, while not needed by ourselves, and the retention of which entails loss of blessing.

Perhaps if there were more of that intense distress for souls that leads to tears, we should more frequently see the results we desire. Sometimes it may be that while we are complaining of the hardness of the hearts of those we are seeking to benefit, the hardness of our own hearts and our feeble apprehension of the solemn reality of eternal things may be the true cause of our want of success.

You must go forward on your knees.

I am so weak that I can hardly write, I cannot read my Bible, I cannot even pray, I can only lie still in God's arms like a little child, and trust.

"The Lord is my shepherd," is on Sunday, is on Monday, and is through every day of the week; is in January, is in December, and every month of the year; is at home, and is in China; is in peace, and, is in war; in abundance, and in penury.

The branch of the vine does not worry, and toil, and rush here to seek for sunshine, and there to find rain. No; it rests in union and communion with the vine; and at the right time, and in the right way, is the right fruit found on it. Let us so abide in the Lord Jesus.

It is the consciousness of the threefold joy of the Lord, His joy in ransoming us, His joy indwelling within us as our Savior and Power for fruit bearing and His joy in possessing us, as His Bride and His delight; it is the consciousness of this joy which is our real strength. Our joy in Him may be a fluctuating thing: His joy in us knows no change.

Since the days of Pentecost, has the whole church ever put aside every other work and waited upon Him for ten days, that the Spirit's power might be manifested? We give too much attention to method and machinery and resources, and too little to the source of power.

There are three indispensable requirements for a missionary: 1. Patience 2. Patience 3. Patience.

It will not do to say that you have no special call to go to China. With these facts before you and with the command of the Lord Jesus to go and preach the gospel to every creature, you need rather to ascertain whether you have a special call to stay at home.

To every toiling, heavy-laden sinner, Jesus says, "Come to me and rest." But there are many toiling, heavy-laden believers, too. For them this same invitation is meant. Note well the words of Jesus, if you are heavy-laden with your service, and do not mistake it. It is not, "Go, labor on," as perhaps you imagine. On the contrary, it is, "Stop, turn back, come to me and rest." Never, never did Christ send a heavy laden one to work; never, never did He send a hungry one, a weary one, a sick, or sorrowing one, away on any service. For such the Bible only says, "Come, come, come."

In Shansi I found Chinese Christians who were accustomed to spend time in fasting and prayer. They recognized that this fasting, which so many dislike, which requires faith in God, since it makes one feel weak and poorly, is really a Divinely appointed means of grace. Perhaps the greatest hindrance to our work is our own imagined strength; and in fasting we learn what poor, weak creatures we are – dependent on a meal of meat for the little strength which we are so apt to lean upon.

Do not work so hard for Christ that you have no strength to pray, for prayer requires strength.

I have seen many men work without praying, though I have never seen any good come out of it; but, I have never seen a man pray without working.

Whatever is your best time in the day, give that to communion with God.

As our Father makes many a flower to bloom unseen in the lonely desert, let us do all that we can do, as under God's eye, though no other eye ever take note of it.

I used to ask God to help me. Then I asked if I might help Him. I ended up by asking Him to do His work through me.

Many Christians estimate difficulties in the light of their own resources, and thus attempt little and often fail in the little they attempt. All God's giants have been weak men who did great things for God because they reckoned on His power and presence with them.

At the timberline where the storms strike with the most fury, the sturdiest trees are found.

All our difficulties are only platforms for the manifestations of His grace, power and love.

The use of means ought not to lessen our faith in God, and our faith in God ought not to hinder our using whatever means He has given us for the accomplishment of His own purposes.

Of course, we all know the scriptural injunctions concerning our vocabulary: "Death and life are in the power of the tongue: and they that love it shall eat the fruit thereof" (Proverbs 18:21), "For by thy words thou shalt be justified, and by thy words thou shalt be condemned" (Matthew 12:37), and "A good man out of the good treasure of his heart bringeth forth that which is good; and an evil man out of the evil treasure of his heart bringeth forth that which is evil: for out of the abundance of the heart his mouth speaketh" (Luke 6:45). Therefore, let us pray along with David, "Let the words of my mouth, and the meditation of my heart, be acceptable in thy sight, O Lord, my strength, and my redeemer" (Psalm 19:14) so that it can be said of us as it was of David, "We having the same spirit of faith, according as it is written, I believed, and therefore have I spoken; we also believe, and therefore speak." (II Corinthians 4:13 – Paul quoting Psalm 116:10)

Eyes

The eyes of an individual become radically different when he receives the anointing of a missionary. Suddenly, he is able to recognize the harvest that he was never able to see even though it was always "right before his eyes."

> Say not ye, There are yet four months, and then cometh harvest? behold, I say unto you, Lift up your eyes, and look on the fields; for they are white already to harvest.
> (John 4:35)

Missionaries see what others look at but do not observe. The average traveler in a country will see the poverty of a country, but not notice the pain in the individual victims. A tourist will look at the pagan temples but fail to observe the emptiness in all the devotees worshiping there. The vacationer will look at the congested traffic and crowded cities and never be aware of the multitude of lost and misdirected souls that make up the masses that populate the cities. This is how we can identify the true missionaries – they see the situations from God's perspective.

Before they are able to see the human situation totally from God's perspective, they must also have their eyesight renewed to a fresh outlook by God Himself. The psalmist expressed this need in his own life when he prayed to God for a vision exam.

> Open thou mine eyes, that I may behold wondrous things out of thy law. (Psalm 119:18)
> Turn away mine eyes from beholding vanity; and quicken thou me in thy way.
> (Psalm 119:37)

He somehow seemed to realize that the changing of his viewpoint was not something that he could do himself. He apparently realized that – just as it takes a supernatural miracle to open the eyes of the physically blind – it would take divine intervention to change his spiritual eyesight as well. Therefore, he asked God to do two things. The first was positive – to give him the ability to see the wondrous things of God. The second was negative – to blind him from seeing the world around him through the emptiness of normal human perception. But he did recognize that he couldn't just toss everything into God's lap. In Psalm 121:1, he confirmed that he would make a determinate decision to focus his own vision, "I will lift up mine eyes unto the hills, from whence cometh my help." Similar to the admonition of Jesus to the Laodicean church that they should come to Him to buy eye salve so that they could see (Revelation 3:18), the psalmist seemed to recognize that the healing would come from the Lord but that he would have to seek for the Lord's intervention just as the Laodiceans would have to make their way to Jesus' apothecary for their ointment.

Perhaps you've found yourself as a mere traveler who sees poverty but not the individual pain, a tourist who sees temples but not the emptiness of the devotees, or a vacationer who sees congestion but not the misdirected souls. If so, you can take a lesson from the psalmist and the Laodiceans and make a visit to the spiritual optometrist. After all, that is the request that the Apostle Paul made for all of us almost two millennia ago, "The eyes of your understanding being enlightened; that ye may know what is the hope of his calling, and what the riches of the glory of his inheritance in the saints." (Ephesians 1:18)

Those who have this kind of eye-opening encounter become men and women who make a real impact upon their world. You may remember that Paul (Saul of Tarsus at the time) was struck blind on the road to Damascus and that the Lord sent His servant Ananias to minister to him so that his sight could be restored. (Acts 9:17-18) But have you ever noticed that it was with those restored eyes that he was able to focus on the spiritual darkness in the soul of Elymas the sorcerer and called forth physical darkness in the form of blindness upon him? "Then Saul, (who also is called Paul,) filled with the Holy Ghost, set his eyes on him." (Acts 13:9) Similarly, we all remember the story of how Peter had to have a supernatural vision to open his eyes to the fact that God wanted to bring the Gentiles into the kingdom (Acts 11:5-11); however, have you ever noticed that when he encountered the lame man at the Beautiful Gate, that his reaction was exactly the same in that he fastened his eyes on the poor invalid (Acts 3:4)? With his new eyesight, Paul was able to discern the demonic influence that was trying to sabotage Sergius Paulus from receiving the gospel – and he was able to deal with that hindrance. Likewise, the determined focus of Peter's eyes allowed him to see beyond the lame man's begging bowl and perceive his real need – and to deal with it.

So it is with those who have a genuine call into ministry, and especially missions ministry – they are able to look beyond the mere symptoms to see the real problems and discern the godly solutions. And one classic case is the story of Anjezë Gonxhe Bojaxhiu (1910 – 1997), a young Albanian girl who dedicated herself to serve as a teacher in Christian school in India. Fascinated by stories of the lives of missionaries and their service in Bengal that she heard as a young child, she was convinced by the age of twelve that she should commit herself to religious life. At the age of eighteen, she joined the Sisters of Loreto in Ireland, to learn English with the view of becoming a missionary teacher at their English-medium school in India. She began her novitiate in Darjeeling where she learned Bengali and taught at St. Teresa's School near her convent. When she was officially inducted into the holy order, she chose to be named after Thérèse de Lisieux, the patron saint of missionaries. After taking her vows as a nun, she began a career as a teacher at the Loreto convent school in eastern Calcutta. Teresa eventually became the headmistress and served in this school for nearly twenty years. Although she enjoyed teaching at the school, she was increasingly disturbed by the poverty surrounding her in Calcutta. As a true missionary, her eyes were open to the anguish of the people – a vision that was intensified as the Bengal famine of 1943 brought misery and death to the city and the August 1946 Direct Action Day began a period of Muslim-Hindu violence.

On September 10, 1946, the devout little nun experienced what she later described as "the call within the call" when she travelled by train to Darjeeling from Calcutta for her annual retreat. "I was to leave the convent and help the poor while living among them. It was an order. To fail would have been to break the faith." Her eyes had led her to a much greater cause than teaching the children of wealthy Indian families and had challenged her to move far beyond the safety of the cloistered walls of the convent. A biographer later wrote, "Though no one knew it at the time, Sister Teresa had just become Mother Teresa."

In 1950, Mother Teresa received the Vatican's permission to initiate – what would eventually become the Missionaries of Charity – an organization to care for "the hungry, the naked, the homeless, the crippled, the blind, the lepers, all those people who feel unwanted, unloved, uncared for throughout society, people that have become a burden to the society and are shunned by everyone." By the time of her death, the thirteen-member Calcutta congregation had grown to more than almost five hundred brothers and over five thousand sisters worldwide, operating more than six hundred missions and schools and shelters in one hundred twenty-three countries where their work included managing orphanages, AIDS hospices, and charity centers that care for refugees, the blind, disabled, aged, alcoholics, the poor and homeless, and victims of floods, epidemics, and famine. In 1982, at the height of the Siege of Beirut, Teresa rescued thirty-seven children trapped in a front-line hospital by brokering a temporary cease-fire between the Israeli army and Palestinian guerrillas. Accompanied by Red Cross workers, she travelled through the war zone to the hospital to evacuate the young patients. She travelled extensively throughout the world to minister to those affected by suffering of all kinds, including the radiation victims at Chernobyl and earthquake victims in Armenia. All this is the fruit of one woman who looked beyond the walls of her convent and saw humans in need.

Before we leave the story of Mother Teresa, we should consider three acts of grace in her ministry. The first was when she received the Nobel Peace Prize in 1979. She refused the conventional ceremonial banquet for laureates, asking that its $192,000 cost be given to the poor in India and saying that earthly rewards were important only if they helped her to help the world's needy. The second came in a meeting of the board of directors for the Missionaries of Charity when she noticed that bottles of water had been placed at each seat. After inquiring how much the organization had paid for each bottle, she insisted that the board members be given glasses of tap water and the money be given to the poor. The last experience I'd like to recall occurred when Mother Teresa was traveling on an airline flight. She requested that her meal be packaged so she could distribute to the needy. Inspired by her act of generosity, passenger after passenger gave up their meals to fed the hungry and the airline established a charitable program to support Mother Teresa's work. All these acts were simple testimonies to the fact that she saw things differently from others around her. It was not because Mother Teresa felt that the kingdom of God was so close to bankruptcy that it couldn't afford to buy bottles of water and feed the hungry at the same time; quite to the contrary, she knew that there was more than enough in the kingdom to supply everyone's need. She simply saw how the eyes of those who have all they need must be opened to the anguish of those who lack.

Ears

The missionary's ears are drastically revolutionized when he is given the honor of serving as God's ambassador to the nations. Now he is able to hear the voice of God within the voices of the ethnic groups of the world as they call out for someone to come bring them the Bread of Life.

> And a vision appeared to Paul in the night; There stood a man of Macedonia, and prayed him, saying, Come over into Macedonia, and help us. And after he had seen the vision, immediately we endeavoured to go into Macedonia, assuredly gathering that the Lord had called us for to preach the gospel unto them. (Acts 16:9-10)

I'd like to quote a couple of lines from a song I learned as a child in Sunday school:

> Be careful little eyes what you see,
> Be careful little ears what you hear.

As Christians, we obviously know that the first and foremost thing which we need to allow to enter our inner man is the Word of God. Jesus said that His words were spirit and life. (John 6:63) If we want life to flow out of our hearts, we must ensure that life is flowing in. The only way to do this is to make sure that we are constantly getting a steady diet of the Word of God. Just one example of the life-giving power in the spoken Word of God can be seen in the vision given to the prophet Ezekiel who was commanded to prophesy to a field of dead bones.

> Again he said unto me, Prophesy upon these bones, and say unto them, O ye dry bones, hear the word of the LORD. Thus saith the Lord GOD unto these bones; Behold, I will cause breath to enter into you,

and ye shall live: And I will lay sinews upon you, and will bring up flesh upon you, and cover you with skin, and put breath in you, and ye shall live; and ye shall know that I am the LORD. So I prophesied as I was commanded: and as I prophesied, there was a noise, and behold a shaking, and the bones came together, bone to his bone. And when I beheld, lo, the sinews and the flesh came up upon them, and the skin covered them above: but there was no breath in them. Then said he unto me, Prophesy unto the wind, prophesy, son of man, and say to the wind, Thus saith the Lord GOD; Come from the four winds, O breath, and breathe upon these slain, that they may live. So I prophesied as he commanded me, and the breath came into them, and they lived, and stood up upon their feet, an exceeding great army. (Ezekiel 37:4-10)

Imagine the power that the Word of God can have in our lives if it can have such a dramatic effect on the totally dead, dismembered, decayed, and dried out corpses of a long-forgotten army. Unfortunately, all too many of us refuse to truly hear and absorb that life-giving Word. In the same context in which Jesus made His proclamation concerning His words being spirit and life, many of His followers turned away because they found His teaching to be too difficult and too demanding. When Jesus turned to His close disciples and asked if they would also abandon Him, Peter responded, "Lord, to whom shall we go? Thou hast the words of eternal life." (John 6:68)

There seem to be several basic hearing problems that plague the human race.

The first one is that we simply can't hear from God because we don't belong to Him. Jesus addressed the religious Jews of His day plainly, "He that is of God heareth God's words: ye therefore hear them not, because ye are not of God." (John 8:47)

The second condition is spelled out in Hebrews 5:11 where the recipients of the letter were addressed as being dull of hearing, "Of whom we have many things to say, and hard to be uttered, seeing ye are dull of hearing." We've all sat through lengthy lectures and seemingly-unending phone calls until we reached the "saturation point" where words seemed to begin to flow in one ear and out the other. We may be able to afford putting our brains in neutral on a few such occasions, but not when it comes to hearing the Word of God. Jesus warned us to be careful about not only what we hear but also about the very way we hear.

> Take heed therefore how ye hear: for whosoever hath, to him shall be given; and whosoever hath not, from him shall be taken even that which he seemeth to have. (Luke 8:18)

We have to be careful as to <u>how</u> we hear because humans have selective processing, the tendency to hear what we want to hear. I've seen this demonstrated time and time again as I've had students giving reviews of the class that I had just taught. It never ceases to amaze me how so many students hear so many things that I never said in the lectures. Their minds were programed to one frequency and they could only hear that particular message no matter what was actually said in the class. One student who was in a number of my classes would always wind up summarizing every lecture with, "Let you light so shine before men so that they can see your good works and glorify your Father who is in heaven" no matter what the topic of the class was actually about. Two people can hear exactly the same thing through two totally different sets of ears. To prove this point, simply ask any husband about his last discussion with his wife — or vice versa.

Perhaps this is the reason that the New Testament repeats the command, "He that hath an ear let him hear," at least fifteen times. God gave us spiritual ears to hear what He is saying to the churches, but it is up to us to keep them tuned in and sensitive to His voice. In the parable of the sower, Jesus demonstrated that the Word of God could be sown into unproductive fields with no lasting result or that it could fall into fertile soil and produce an abundant harvest. Interestingly enough, He concludes His remarks with one of the admonitions concerning having listening ears, implying that the ear is the key to having the productive soil for the Word of God. (Luke 8:8)

A missionary friend of mine in the Dominican Republic had a problem with the portable generator he needed for a crusade he was doing. When none of the local mechanics could figure what was wrong with the machine, my friend resorted to calling a friend of his on the cell phone. By simply listening over the phone to the sound that the generator was making, the friend was able to diagnose the problem with the generator and explain to the missionary what needed to be done to get it working properly. Now that's what I call an attentive ear.

God is looking for people with that same kind of spiritual hearing. That's why He insisted to each of the seven churches in Revelation at if anyone has an ear he should hear what the Spirit is saying. In addition, He gave us that same admonition at least nine times during His earthly ministry. (Matthew 11:15, 13:9, 43; Mark 4:9, 23, 7:16, 8:18; Luke 8:8, 14:35)

The third hindrance to hearing the Word of God is that sometimes we simply don't want to hear it! Let's look at the story of the giving of the Ten Commandments in Exodus chapter twenty. Verse one plainly states that God orally spoke the Decalogue in the hearing of the entire camp of Israel. However, if we continue the story as it is recorded further on in the chapter we will see that the people begged Moses to become an intermediary between them and God. They did not want to continue hearing directly from the very mouth of God. Instead, they devised a plan wherein Moses would hear the direct voice of God and then communicate His messages to them second-hand. They simply did not want the responsibility of hearing directly from God. I assume that they – just as we often tend to be – were more comfortable with a second-hand gospel because they knew that there might be a margin of error if it passed through a human channel – giving then an excuse for continuing in their unrighteousness. On the other hand, if they heard from the divine source directly, they would be without an excuse.

> And all the people saw the thunderings, and the lightnings, and the noise of the trumpet, and the mountain smoking: and when the people saw it, they removed, and stood afar off. And they said unto Moses, Speak thou with us, and we will hear: but let not God speak with us, lest we die. And Moses said unto the people, Fear not: for God is come to prove you, and that his fear may be before your faces, that ye sin not. And the people stood afar off, and Moses drew near unto the thick darkness where God was. And the LORD said unto Moses, Thus thou shalt say unto the children of Israel, Ye have seen that I have talked with you from heaven. (verses 18-22; also see Deuteronomy 5:22-27 and 18:16)

The fourth complication is that we often can't recognize God's voice when He speaks to us. The lad Samuel had this difficulty when God first spoke to him. In the third chapter of I Samuel we find the story of how the Lord called him three times before he finally recognized that it was God Himself calling rather than his mentor Eli. However, if we read the rest of the story, we will see that Samuel developed an exceptionally clear ability to recognize the voice of the Lord. He became known as a "seer" because he could hear the whisperings of God concerning even the most secret of divine mysteries. In fact, the people of the region actually developed a fear of him, always cognizant that he might "read their mail" and expose the "skeletons in their closets" or reveal the "dust that they had swept under the carpet."

As in the case with the people of Samuel's day who were afraid that he might reveal their transgressions and shortcomings, the fifth reason why we cannot hear the voice of God is because we are simply afraid. This has been a common problem since "day one." It was fear that drove Adam and Eve into hiding and away from their daily time of fellowship and conversation with God. (Genesis 3:8-10)

The sixth problem we have in not being able to hear the Lord is that we often do not give diligence to what we hear. In Exodus 15:26, the Lord – speaking concerning our health and healing – said that we must diligently hearken to His voice and give ear to His commandments in order to partake of His divine provision. While Deuteronomy chapter fifteen speaks of release from financial and physical bondage, verse five limits these provisions to only those who will carefully hearken unto the voice of the Lord and observe all His commandments. The twenty-eighth chapter of the book contains an oft-quoted roster of blessings, but we must realize that the opening two verses limit these benefits only to those who hearken diligently unto the voice of the Lord and that verse fifteen turns all the blessings into curses for those who will not hearken unto His voice and observe all His commandments and statutes. For just a minute, let's think on totally natural terms. Suppose you ask someone for directions to a specific place. Imagine that the instructions are a bit complicated with several turns, some to the left and some to the right. If you listen with only a casual ear, you will likely make the first turn with no difficulty and possibly take the second turn correctly; however, by the time you are at the third crossroad, you will be confused as to which way to turn. You'll probably be totally lost before reaching the fourth road. Unfortunately, we are all too satisfied with turning a nonchalant ear to God and, therefore, missing the precise plan He wants to lay out for our lives. Think of the detail that God gave Moses when He laid out the plans for the Old Testament Tabernacle; it took seven full chapters of Exodus (chapters 25-31) to spell out the pattern for the structure and the priestly order. But, more importantly, notice the preciseness with which Moses followed each detail when he implemented the blueprint. (chapters 36-40) The reward for this attention to detail was an invasion of the presence of the Lord so overwhelming that Moses was not even able to enter the Tabernacle. (Exodus 40:34-35)

      Allow me to share the story of one man whose ears were opened in a miraculous way. Adoniram Judson (1788 – 1850) was a pastor's son, yet he resisted the message of salvation the whole time he lived in the Christian home. When he went away to study at Providence College (later to become Brown University), he became close friends with a skeptic named Jacob Eames. Because he was brought up in a religious home, Judson initially resisted Eames' attacks on Christianity, but eventually became overwhelmed by the logic of Eames' atheism and eventually declared himself an atheist as well – an announcement that, of course, left his parents heart-broken but undeterred in their prayers. Indulging in every form of unrestrained sin, Adoniram drove his father's theological arguments out of his mind, but he could not forget his mother's tears as he pursued his ambitions in New York City and then began a westward adventure. On the first night of his journey, Judson stopped at a small inn where there was only one empty bed – in a room that was divided by a curtain so that two guests could share the room but still have some semblance of privacy. Unfortunately, the guest in the shared accommodation was deathly ill and groaned in agony the whole night. There were also the constant footsteps of the dying man's attendants and the creaking of loose floorboards. Eventually there was one final gasp for breath from the man on the other side of the curtain. Being that close to death rekindled some of his father's words concerning heaven and hell. The young "atheist" questioned if the man in the next room might not be prepared for death. But more unsettling was his concern if he himself was ready to face "eternity." There was a terror in these fantastically unwinding ideas. But as they presented themselves, another part of himself jeered. Certainly, these imaginations were nothing more than midnight fancies and emotional responses to a traumatic situation he had just lived through. Undoubtedly, these questioning thoughts were only skin-deep intrusions challenging the freethinking philosophy of Adoniram Judson – valedictorian, scholar, teacher, ambitious man, and atheist! He shrank back at the very thought of what his classmates at the university would say to these terrors of the night and how they robbed the boldness out of his courageous defiance of religion. Above all, Adoniram could only imagine how his clear-headed, skeptical, witty, and talented friend Eames would laugh him to shame. But eventually it was morning, and as the sunlight through his window dispelled the darkness of the night, so also his apprehensions vanished. He dressed and ran downstairs, looking for the innkeeper so he could pay his room bill. As he handed over the money, Judson casually asked, "Do you know who the gentleman who died last night was?" The reply came back, "Oh, yes, a young man from the college in Providence – Eames, Jacob Eames." How he got through the next few hours, Adoniram was never to remember. Only the words, "Lost, lost, lost," echoed through his mind. The truth of scripture struck deep in his heart. He knew then that his father was right. He knew Eames was lost! Lost for eternity!

Because of what Adoniram Judson heard that night, he gave his life to Christ and to study of the scripture. Later he heard the Lord's call to ministry and to missions. As the first missionary to be sent out from America, he sailed to Calcutta, India, where he was baptized by immersion by the great missions pioneer William Carey. Since this was a theological break with the denomination that was sponsoring him, Judson resigned and then set sail for Burma to become the first missionary to that nation.

But blessed are your eyes, for they see: and
your ears, for they hear. (Matthew 13:16)

Feet

Missionaries have beautiful feet to allow them to go to the nations of the world to preach (Mark 16:15) and teach the Word of God (Matthew 28:19).

How beautiful upon the mountains are the feet of him that bringeth good tidings, that publisheth peace; that bringeth good tidings of good, that publisheth salvation; that saith unto Zion, Thy God reigneth! (Isaiah 52:7)
The Bible is full of promises concerning the feet of the righteous:
Their feet are secured and established.
He maketh my feet like hinds' feet, and setteth me upon my high places. (Psalm 18:33)
Thou hast enlarged my steps under me, that my feet did not slip. (Psalm 18:36)
And hast not shut me up into the hand of the enemy: thou hast set my feet in a large room. (Psalm 31:8)
He brought me up also out of an horrible pit, out of the miry clay, and set my feet upon a rock, and established my goings. (Psalm 40:2)
For thou hast delivered my soul from death: wilt not thou deliver my feet from falling, that I may walk before God in the light of the living? (Psalm 56:13)
Which holdeth our soul in life, and suffereth not our feet to be moved. (Psalm 66:9)
For thou hast delivered my soul from death, mine eyes from tears, and my feet from falling. (Psalm 116:8)
Their feet victoriously vanquish their

enemies.

I have wounded them that they were not able to rise: they are fallen under my feet. (Psalm 18:38)

He shall subdue the people under us, and the nations under our feet. (Psalm 47:3)

Thou shalt tread upon the lion and adder: the young lion and the dragon shalt thou trample under feet. (Psalm 91:13)

And the God of peace shall bruise Satan under your feet shortly. The grace of our Lord Jesus Christ be with you. Amen. (Romans 16:20)

For he must reign, till he hath put all enemies under his feet. (I Corinthians 15:25)

For he hath put all things under his feet. But when he saith all things are put under him, it is manifest that he is excepted, which did put all things under him. (I Corinthians 15:27)

And hath put all things under his feet, and gave him to be the head over all things to the church, (Ephesians 1:22)

Thou hast put all things in subjection under his feet. For in that he put all in subjection under him, he left nothing that is not put under him. But now we see not yet all things put under him. (Hebrews 2:8)

      Their feet declare the Lord's protection. And saith unto him, If thou be the Son of God, cast thyself down: for it is written, He shall give his angels charge concerning thee: and in their hands they shall bear thee up, lest at any time thou dash thy foot against a stone. (Matthew 4:6)

And in their hands they shall bear thee up, lest

at any time thou dash thy foot against a stone. (Luke 4:11)

    Their feet are directed by the Lord.

Thy word is a lamp unto my feet, and a light unto my path. (Psalm 119:105)

Our feet shall stand within thy gates, O Jerusalem. (Psalm 122:2)

To give light to them that sit in darkness and in the shadow of death, to guide our feet into the way of peace. (Luke 1:79)

Their feet declare judgment against those who reject the gospel.

And whosoever shall not receive you, nor hear your words, when ye depart out of that house or city, shake off the dust of your feet. (Matthew 10:14)

And whosoever shall not receive you, nor hear you, when ye depart thence, shake off the dust under your feet for a testimony against them. Verily I say unto you, It shall be more tolerable for Sodom and Gomorrha in the day of judgment, than for that city. (Mark 6:11)

And whosoever will not receive you, when ye go out of that city, shake off the very dust from your feet for a testimony against them. (Luke 9:5)

But they shook off the dust of their feet against them, and came unto Iconium. (Acts 13:51)

    Their feet symbolize submission to the Lord.

And laid them down at the apostles' feet: and distribution was made unto every man according as he had need. (Acts 4:35)

Having land, sold it, and brought the money, and laid it at the apostles' feet. (Acts 4:37)

Their feet determine possession.
Every place whereon the soles of your feet shall tread shall be yours: from the wilderness and Lebanon, from the river, the river Euphrates, even unto the uttermost sea shall your coast be. (Deuteronomy 11:24)
Every place that the sole of your foot shall tread upon, that have I given unto you, as I said unto Moses. (Joshua 1:3)
But most importantly, their feet are for spreading the gospel.
And how shall they preach, except they be sent? as it is written, How beautiful are the feet of them that preach the gospel of peace, and bring glad tidings of good things! (Romans 10:15)
And your feet shod with the preparation of the gospel of peace. (Ephesians 6:15)

Eric Liddell (1902 – 1945) is an outstanding example of a man whose feet were beautiful in proclaiming the gospel. Best known from the movie Chariots of Fire, Liddle was the Olympic athlete who refused to run in a Sunday competition due his religious beliefs. However, the rest of his story takes him back to China (the land of his birth as the son of a missionary couple) where he used his place of prominence as an athletic celebrity to share the gospel, into concentration camp, and the death of a war prisoner.

Eric was born in Tientsin, China, the second son of the Reverend and Mrs. James Dunlop Liddell, Scottish missionaries with the London Missionary Society. Liddell went to school in China until the age of six, at which point he was sent to boarding school in London. While at Edinburgh University, Liddell became well known for being the fastest runner in Scotland and was nicknamed the

"Flying Scotsman." Newspapers carried stories of his feats at track meets, and many articles stated that he was a potential Olympic winner. While in college, he became a recognized speaker at evangelical events which drew large crowds of young men because of his athletic accomplishments. In the 1924 Summer Olympics in Paris, Liddell refused to run in a heat held on Sunday and was forced to withdraw from the hundred-meter race, his best event. Instead, he competed in the four-hundred-meter race and achieved a record time that was not broken for the next twelve years.

Liddell returned to Northern China to serve as a missionary, where he taught in the mission school and used his athletic abilities to train and inspire the students. The area where he was serving become a particularly treacherous battleground with the invading Japanese. Missionaries were likely to be shot without question. Eric discussed it with his wife and though it was hard to leave, he knew he was the best person to go. Eric Liddell worked long hours traveling in the war-torn area preaching and tending the sick. Many times, he had to carry the injured to the hospital on his bike over rough roads while dodging gunfire. Sometimes it would take an entire day to get to the village hospital. In the meantime, the Japanese were taking over more of the country and eventually took over his mission station. Eric was interred in a concentration camp along with the members of the China Inland Mission and many other Christians. Even during his incarceration, Eric organized games and events to encourage the young men in the camp. In his last letter to his wife, written on the day he died, Liddell wrote of suffering a nervous breakdown due to overwork. He actually had an inoperable brain tumor; overwork and malnourishment may have hastened his death.

Hands

Missionaries have special hands because they are particularly blessed by God to serve others and do miracles.

And these signs shall follow them that believe; In my name shall they cast out devils; they shall speak with new tongues; They shall take up serpents; and if they drink any deadly thing, it shall not hurt them; they shall lay hands on the sick, and they shall recover. (Mark 16:17-18)

T.L. Osborn (1923 – 2013) first went to India as an on-fire and determined missionary; however, he soon realized that he lacked something necessary to reach the unbelievers of India. When he discovered that the Muslims believed in one God and had a book that they held as scared as the Christians do their Bible, he was was totally disillusioned and slipped away from the mission compound in the dead of night. "With his tail tucked between his hind legs," he returned to the USA and began to question if he could ever be a missionary and have an impact among unbelievers. However, all that changed in one night when he sat in the upper balcony at a healing crusade directed by William Braham. As miracle after miracle occurred on the main platform, the Holy Spirit spoke to T.L., "You can do THAT! You can DO that! You CAN do that! YOU can do that!" After receiving the empowerment of the Holy Spirit, T.L. and his wife Daisy returned to the mission field and over the course of the next five decades traveled to more than seventy countries and reached millions of people in crusades that often numbered into the tens of thousands in attendance.

Every meeting was accompanied by miracles of biblical proportions. They created prolific quantities of evangelistic and training materials, some of which were translated into more than one hundred thirty languages. Under his influence, more than one hundred fifty thousand churches were birthed.

Knees

The knees of missionaries are especially adapted to prayer in that they have a two-fold prayer mandate: 1) for the nations to come to the Lord and 2) that more come join them in the mission harvest fields.

> Ask of me, and I shall give thee the heathen for thine inheritance, and the uttermost parts of the earth for thy possession. (Psalm 2:8)
> Therefore said he unto them, The harvest truly is great, but the labourers are few: pray ye therefore the Lord of the harvest, that he would send forth labourers into his harvest. (Luke 10:2)

Prayer is always a characteristic of those who sincerely desire to see their world won to the Lord. Samuel determined that he would not cease his intercession on the behalf of Israel even when they rejected his leadership. (I Samuel 12:23) Abraham interceded for the wicked cities of Sodom and Gomorrah. (Genesis 18:23-32) Moses was willing to give his own life in intercession for his people. (Exodus 32:32) Jeremiah wept for the people of Israel. (Jeremiah 3:21) Ezekiel sought for a man to stand in the gap and fill in the hedge of protection and intercession for the people. (Ezekiel 22:30) Paul was willing to abandon his own salvation if it could have rescued the Jews. (Romans 9:3) Of course, Jesus' life was one of prayer. (Matthew 23:37; Luke 6:12-13, 22:31-32) The apostles gave themselves to prayer (Acts 2:42, 6:1-4) with Paul serving essentially as the "poster boy" of prayer (I Corinthians 1:4, Philippians 1:3-4, Colossians 1:3, I Thessalonians 1:2, II Thessalonians 1:3, I Timothy 1:2, II Timothy 1:3, Philemon

1:4). However, it is in Paul's letter to the Romans that we see the overwhelming role of intercession in his ministry. Even calling upon God as a witness to the integrity of his claim, Paul writes of constant prayers on the behalf of a church he has never visited and in which he has very few personal contacts. (Romans 1:9) This is the quality that marks a true missionary

John Hyde (1865 – 1912) was an extraordinary man of prayer who became known as "Praying Hyde" in India, his mission field, and the world. It has been said of him that "the Spirit made him an object-lesson to us, that we might have a better idea of what was Christ's prayer-life."

John's father, a Presbyterian minister, would frequently pray for laborers to be sent into the harvest. The result was that three of their six kids were sent as an answer to that prayer. When his brother died as the result of a sickness he contracted on the mission field, John determined to take his brother's place on the mission field. His enthusiasm inspired over half of his classmates in the seminary to become missionaries.

His first few years in India were fruitless and discouraging as he struggled in his language studies due to a hearing impairment. Eventually, he decided to resign and return home; however, the people in his village countered with, "If you never speak the language of our lips, you speak the language of our hearts." With that, he decided to stay. John would spend hours and hours with his Lord – forgetting about sleep and food – in the gap for believers and those to be saved. "Oh God, give me souls or I die!" would become one of his most famous prayers. However, his coworkers, feeling that John was negligent in his physical ministry because he devoted so much of his time to Bible study and prayer, accused him of being fanatical and extreme. Because he would even spend whole days and nights in prayer, John became known as "the man who never sleeps."

God's fire was burning in John's heart so intensely that his constant prayer was that he would rather burn out than rust out was already being answered."

Along with the help of a fellow missionary, McCheyne Paterson, John Hyde, planned a convention for the deepening of the spiritual life of the local people. The two missionaries prayed for thirty days before the convention started. Nine days into the intercession, a third missionary joined them for the final twenty-one days of night-and-day petition for a mighty outpouring of the power of God. In answer to their prayers, the Holy Spirit came down, convicted of sin and many lives were changed. The missionaries came to a new consecration to the will of God, and the work took on a new dimension, resulting in a rapid extension of the kingdom of God – forever changing the spiritual landscape of India. Thousands of lives were touched and transformed. It has been said that the victory of these meetings was not won in the pulpit but in the closet. Often the glory rested on these meetings in a mighty way, while hidden out of sight, John Hyde and a faithful few travailed in prayer. God called him to be a watchman and took him he even deeper into intercession for the church and the lost.

Even though John spent much of his time in prayer, he was a very relational person, cheerful and loving, always concerned for others. He would grasp every opportunity to share Jesus with other people. As a personal worker he would engage a man in a talk about his salvation. By and by he would have his hands on the man's shoulders, be looking him very earnestly in the eye. Soon he would get the man on his knees, confessing his sins and seeking salvation. Such a one he would baptize in the village, by the roadside, or anywhere.

John's prayer life inspired many people who had the honor of coming into God's presence together with him, and changed their lives forever. One man describes this encounter, "He came to my room, turned the key in the door, dropped on his knees, waited five minutes without a single syllable coming from his lips. I could hear my own heart thumping and beating. I felt the hot tears running down my face. I knew I was with God. Then with upturned face, down which the tears were streaming, he said, "Oh, God!" Then for five minutes at least, he was still again, and then when he knew he was talking with God his arm went around my shoulder and there came up from the depth of his heart such petitions for men as I had never heard before. I rose from my knees to know what real prayer was."

Heart

The heart of a missionary has been uniquely touched by God so that he cares enough about a lost and dying world that he is willing to sacrifice his own comforts and aspirations in order to make a difference in the lives of men, women, children, and societies around the world. In what has become a landmark prayer of missions, the founder of World Vision Bob Pierce succinctly summarized the heart of a true missionary, "Let my heart be broken with the things that break God's heart." But this is not just the prayer of just one humanitarian; it is the motivation of every person who has encountered the heart of the Savior and is compelled to penetrate the world with the love and gospel of Jesus Christ.

> I have found David the son of Jesse, a man after mine own heart, which shall fulfil all my will. (Acts 13:22)

In Jesus we see the heart of a missionary when He wept over the city of Jerusalem (Matthew 23:37), promised to lay down His life for the flock (John 10:15), and prayed for the very men who were crucifying Him (Luke 23:34). Paul displayed this same heart when he told the Corinthians that he was willing to spend and be spent for their benefit (II Corinthians 12:15) and that he would even give up his own salvation if it were possible to win the Jewish people to Christ (Romans 9:3).

There are probably no better examples of the missionary heart for the nations than the testimonies of Jim (1927 – 1956) and Elizabeth (1926 – 2015) Elliot. The son of a traveling preacher with the Plymouth Brethren church, Jim professed faith in Jesus at the age of six. In school, Jim was recognized as a gifted orator who frequently used the scriptures and his Christian faith as the foundations for his speeches.

His first missionary exposure was linguistic studies with the Wycliffe translators. It was here that he first learned of the Huaorani (also called the "Auca," the Quichua word for "savage"), a group of Ecuadorian indigenous people considered to be violent and dangerous to outsiders. Although many friends and family members encouraged Jim to use his skills as a youth pastor in the US, Jim considering the home church "well-fed" and determined that international missions should take precedence. After first considering a work in India, Jim eventually decided to partner with his friend Bill Cathers to go to Ecuador. However, two months later Cathers informed him that he planned to marry, making it impossible for him to accompany Elliot as they had planned. Instead, Elliot spent the winter and spring of 1951 working with his friend Ed McCully in Chester, Illinois, running a radio program, preaching in prisons, holding evangelistic rallies, and teaching Sunday school. When McCully married later that summer, Jim partnered with Pete Fleming, and began to make plans to move to Ecuador. In the meantime, Jim made a visit to Elisabeth, who had been a classmate and close friend during college. In his journal he expressed hope that they would be able to be married, but at the same time felt that he was called to go to Ecuador without her. In October of 1953, one and a half years after his arrival in Ecuador, Jim and Elisabeth were married in a simple civil ceremony held in Quito.

Jim and four other missionaries – Ed McCully, Roger Youderian, Pete Fleming, and their pilot, Nate Saint – made contact from their Piper PA-14 airplane with the Huaorani using a loudspeaker and a basket to pass down gifts. After several months, the men decided to make physical contact with the Huaorani by landing their plane on a little strip of beach along the Curaray River not far from their village.

They were approached one time by a small group of Huaorani and even gave an airplane ride to one curious Huaorani whom they called "George" (his real name was Naenkiwi). Encouraged by these friendly encounters, they began plans to visit the Huaorani, without knowing that Naenkiwi had lied to the others about the missionaries' intentions. Even though Jim carried a gun with him, he had determined that it would only be used to fire warning shots to scare off any attackers.   When a group of Huaorani warriors did attack, Jim did not defend himself and the entire missionary party was speared to death on January 8, 1956.

His journal entry for October 28, 1949, expresses his belief that work dedicated to Jesus was more important than his life, "He is no fool who parts with that which he cannot keep, when he is sure to be recompensed with that which he cannot lose."

Even though Jim died in his attempt to reach the Huaorani people with the gospel, the true heart for the nations was demonstrated by Elizabeth when she took their young daughter and moved to the village of the very people who killed her husband. She lived with them for a number of years until the tribe (including the assassins who took her husband's life) came to Christ.

Mouth

We began our study of the characteristics of a missionary by looking at their language and vocabulary; however, I'd like to end this study with looking at the missionary's mouth itself. It is through the mouth that the missionary actually demonstrates the heart that is inside him (Matthew 12:34) – one of courage, faith, and anointing – or one of fear, mediocrity, and unbelief. The Apostle Paul encouraged the Ephesian believers to be strong in the Lord and to put on the whole armor of God so that they could become powerful men and women of God with the mission as prayer warriors. And then he zeroed in on one request that they pray for his mouth because it was with his mouth that he was able to fulfill his missionary ministry.

> Praying…for me…that I may open my mouth boldly, to make known the mystery of the gospel for which I am an ambassador in bonds: that therein I may speak boldly, as I ought to speak. (Ephesians 6:18-20)

The story of William Carey (1761 –1834) is one of the most inspiring of all those who used their mouths to change the world. Carey spoke boldly to convince the Western Church to send missionaries to the unreached world, to share the gospel with the non-Christians of India, and to convince the government to make powerful social changes in the culture.

Carey spent his hours as he worked at his cobbler's bench mending shoes to pray over a world map that he had posted on the wall. By 1787, he became so burdened for the lost of the world that he approached the British Baptist Association with the question of whether it was the duty of all Christians to spread the gospel. The retort that came back was, "Young man, sit down; when God pleases to convert the heathen, he will do it without your aid and mine." However, after persistent persuasion and the presentation of his groundbreaking missionary manifesto <u>An Enquiry into the Obligations of Christians to Use Means for the Conversion of the Heathens</u>, Carey was commissioned as the first Protestant foreign missionary in 1792 and became known as the Father of Modern Protestant Missions. As soon as funds were raised, he set sail for Calcutta, India, where he invested the rest of his life. Although he and his team produced only about seven hundred converts, they left behind a legacy of a transformed India by:

1. translating the Bible into thirty-four Asian languages
2. compiling dictionaries of Sanskrit, Marathi, Panjabi, and Telegu
3. founding the still influential Serampore College
4. establishing churches and nineteen mission stations
5. planting more than one hundred rural schools
6. encouraging the education of girls
7. starting the Horticultural Society of India
8. serving as a professor at Fort William College
9. beginning the weekly publication <u>The Friend of India</u>
10. printing the first Indian newspaper
11. introducing the concept of the savings bank to assist poor farmers
12. fighting against sati, the burning of widows

Conclusion

Take a look at your skin color, language, eyes, ears, feet, hands, knees, heart, and mouth and see if perhaps God has been molding you into a missionary. Remember one important lesson: Missionaries are not made by crossing the sea, but by seeing the cross. If your eyes, ears, feet, hands, knees, and heart indicate that you are a missionary, you are a missionary – even if you never leave your hometown. If you have seen the cross, you are a missionary – even if your field is your own family, friends, and people who speak your own language and have the same color of skin that you do.

When Jesus cast the demon out of Legion, he wanted to travel with Jesus and become a missionary with Him. Jesus' response was that this young man's mission field was his own familiar territory. (Mark 5:19, Luke 8:39) Certainly his eyes, ears, feet, hands, knees, and heart had all the telltale signs of a missionary.

Teach All Nations Mission

Teach All Nations Mission (TAN) is a global evangelical educational ministry birthed from the teaching ministries of Delron and Peggy Shirley. The name for Teach All Nations Mission was chosen to carefully indicate the exact heart of the Shirleys' mission. TAN's commitment is to establish a solid foundation in national pastors and leaders so they can help enrich their own people. This vision is being accomplished by holding national leadership conferences and publishing and distributing Christian teaching materials in English and their local languages.

Someone accurately observed concerning the revival that is occurring in many parts of our world today that it is a mile wide but only an inch deep – the result of energetic evangelism by both missionaries and local Christians. Sadly, there is a marked shortage of teachers who are taking the next step in fulfilling our Lord's directive to teach them how to observe all that He has commanded. Therefore, Teach All Nations Mission has literally taken the words of Christ from Matthew 28:19, "Teach all nations," as its motto and mission statement.

TAN's commitment is to deepen that revival by training the pastors and leaders who then go back and strengthen their congregations. TAN pays for the travel and lodging of handpicked leaders because Delron and Peggy want to invest into their lives but know that these third-world saints could never afford to come at their own expense. TAN always provides the meals for all the guests during these conferences. The ministry also furnishes solid Christian literature in their local language or in English for those who understand the language.

Delron and Peggy realize that the challenge is much bigger than what they can accomplish in person; therefore, they have determined to expand the scope of their vision. One area of expansion includes a scholarship fund that will allow selected individuals to obtain formal education in solid Christian colleges and Bible schools or through correspondence courses. The ministry has also assisted in building a Christian school in Zimbabwe and a Bible college in Nepal. Additionally, Teach All Nations assists the pastors and leaders they work with in times of need such as the tsunami in Sri Lanka, the earthquake in Nepal, and hurricanes in Belize and in the Turks and Caicos Islands.

     Your gifts to and prayers for Teach All Nations will help the Shirleys continue their outreach to Christian leadership around the world.

Teach All Nations Mission
3210 Cathedral Spires
Colorado Springs, CO 8904
719-685-9999
www.teachallnationsmission.com
teachallnations@msn.com

Books by Delron & Peggy Shirley
available at www.teachallnationsmission.com

Bingo – A Fresh Look at Grace

An old joke tells of a man who stood at the Pearly Gates recounting all his good deeds in an effort to gain entry into Paradise. When Saint Peter tallied up the gentleman's score, he did not have anywhere near enough points to qualify. His knee-jerk reaction to the count was, "I'll never get in except by the grace of God." At that instant, the gates swung open and Saint Peter graciously welcomed the gentleman inside. We all know that it is only through grace that we will ever inherit the kingdom of God, but how much do we understand about this all-important subject? Join Bible teacher Delron Shirley as he explores the biblical principle of grace and investigates some of the misconceptions that are current in the Body of Christ today.

Christmas Thoughts

Christmas. The very mention of the word fills our hearts and heads with thoughts – joyous memories, visions of childhood delights, scenes of family gatherings, smells of fresh pastries, tastes of delicious holiday treats, recollections of special friends, strains of favorite carols, and "warm fuzzies" of evergreens, mistletoe, roaring fires, fancy wrappings, shiny decorations, and happy faces. Yes, Christmas is all about thoughts. And we invite you to snuggle up with a hot chocolate and delve into our thoughts about Christmas – and the Christ child whose coming we are celebrating.

Cornerstones of Faith

In our Christian faith, there are also some important cornerstones which serve as foundations to bear the weight of the life we are to build upon them, as indicators or identifiers of who we are as believers, as ceremonial testimonies to the fact that our lives are being built upon Christ, and an unquestionable and invariable standards against which to test and measure everything else in our lives. Proper attention to these essential cornerstones of our faith ensure that our lives rest upon a firm foundation so that we will not fail or falter. Join Dr. Delron Shirley in an examination of the foundation on which our lives must be built.

Daily Devotional Bible Study (five volumes)

This five-volume set of studies takes you on a four-year journey through the Bible. Each manual consists of a walk through the scripture based on studying one chapter each weekday for the fifty-two weeks in a year. Each daily entry includes one verse to memorize. Next comes a short distillation of the basic principle of the chapter and a brief outline of the chapter. This study is intended to be of a rather devotional approach. The Bible study is followed by a simple prayer intended to bring the truth of the chapter into practical application. A section for the reader's notes follows where you can log your own personal revelations and insights about the chapter. A space for logging your own personal spiritual journal (which could include prayer requests, answered prayers, and testimonies) rounds out the daily devotion. The entries for the weekends are a similar format for a study through Psalms. Just twenty minutes a day, seven days a week, fifty-two weeks a year will produce one brand new man in each individual who seriously applies himself to the program and the program to himself.

Daily Ditties from Delron's Desk (Six issues are available**)**

Each new day comes with its own challenges and blessings. In Daily Ditties from Delron's Desk, you'll enjoy a little pick-me-up to get your day started. So sit back with a warm cup of coffee or tea and see what is in store for you today.

Lessons from the Life of David

In 2004, Michelangelo's famous sculpture, David, went through an extensive cleaning and restoration process in celebration of its five-hundredth birthday. Half a millennium of grime has been removed to once again reveal the majestic splendor with which the masterpiece sparkled when it was first placed in the Piazza Signoria in Florence, Italy. This famous marble statue has often been noted as a most perfect depiction of the human body. And we often think of its subject – the biblical David – as being perfect as well. However, the wonderful thing about the Bible is that it tells the truth -- even about its greatest heroes. They are presented to us as uncovered as Michelangelo's subject, with the only difference being that the Bible depicts its subjects with all their warts, mid-rib bulges, scars, and other defects. In Lessons from the Life of David, Bible teacher Delron Shirley explores both David's triumphs and failures in order to find valuable lessons for our own lives for today.

The Great Commission – DOABLE

While traversing the teeming streets of Kathmandu, Nepal, missionary teacher Delron Shirley was overwhelmed with the throngs of people who had not yet heard the gospel of Jesus Christ. Looking out at the myriad of faces, it seemed like an impossible task to reach them all. Yet, he knew that Jesus' directive was that the gospel be taken to every human—not just in this one city, but on the entire planet. If reaching this one city seemed like a gargantuan challenge, reaching the planet was beyond imagination! Join Delron in his quest through the scriptures as he explores why the Bible promises that the Great Commission can actually be accomplished and how it is doable in our generation.

Dr. Livingstone, I Presume

Probably the most famous quote in all the annals of missionary history is the greeting of newsman and adventurer Henry Stanley when he finally reached missionary and explorer David Livingstone in the remote interior of Africa, "Dr. Livingstone, I presume?" In this little study based on that historic encounter, Bible teacher and missionary Dr. Delron Shirley considers how we can really pick out who is a missionary. His real hope is that you can find yourself in these few short pages and join the call to fulfill the Great Commission of bringing the gospel of Jesus Christ to the whole world in this generation.

Finally, My Brethren

"Finally, my brethren," these are words that seem all too familiar to us when we think of putting on the armor of God for spiritual warfare. However, we often miss the real impact of Paul's message to the church because we have used this as our starting point. But just as we don't start at the top step when we climb a ladder, we can't begin our preparation for spiritual warfare at the last step – putting on the armor. In fact, the Apostle Paul gave us more than fifty steps of preparation to complete before we are ready to get dressed for battle. Join Delron Shirley as he uncovers these often neglected truths. Discover life-transforming truths about your enemy, yourself, God, who you are in Christ, who Christ is in you, and your position in the struggle between the powers of heaven and hell.

Going Deeper in Jesus

In this seventy-three-day devotional volume, Bible teacher Delron Shirley invites you to go with him on a quest into the Jesus treasure chest to discover the unimaginable gifts that God has made available to us in Christ.

The IN Factors

It was offering time in the Sunday school class, and the teacher directed the children to quote a Bible verse about giving as they dropped in their nickels and dimes. A little Afro-American girl with her hair in meticulously cornrow braids grinned from ear to ear as she dropped in the first coin and quoted, "It is more blessed to give than to receive." Her redheaded, freckle-faced friend shyly blushed as she added to the coffer while mumbling, "Give and it shall be given back to you." Next, a young guy tossed in what might have been his "tooth fairy money" as he flashed a broad smile that exposed the spot where his front tooth had been last Sunday. He then recited, "The Lord loves a cheerful giver." As the fourth little fellow stumbled through, "The seed in the good soil brought forth thirty-, sixty-, and one-hundred-fold return," the teacher anxiously eyed the next child – a first-time visitor who had not been schooled in any of the "giving" passages. Anxious over the fact that the guest would be embarrassed, her heart raced a bit as the offering basket reached him. As the reluctant little tyke begrudgingly plunked in his contribution, he blurted out, "A fool and his money are soon parted."

Although the visitor's quote wasn't from the Bible, it was apparently more appropriate in his own case than any of the verses with which the teacher had coached the rest of the pupils. The truth is that most of us, like the students in the elementary class, have been taught only part of the lesson of what God wants us to know about finances. In <u>The IN Factors</u>, Bible teacher Delron Shirley invites you to join him as he explores some of the lessons that have been taught – but equally important – truths on the topic.

In This Sign Conquer

Marching toward an enemy that he wasn't sure he could defeat, Constantine questioned himself, his army, his military abilities, and even his deities. Then suddenly something happened that changed his life. No, something happened that changed the whole history of Western civilization. He saw a vision in the sky of the Christian cross accompanied by the words, "In this sign conquer." Abandoning his pagan gods and accepting the cross of Christ as his battle insignia, he marched into the Battle of Malvian, defeated Maxentius, and took the throne of the Roman Empire. Since none of us was there in AD 312, we can't be certain how sincere the new emperor was in his acceptance of the cross as his victory symbol. However, we must know that there are signs and symbols that God has given to each of us to ensure our victory and success in life. Join Bible teacher Delron Shirley as he explores this fascinating topic.

Interface

This book should be viewed as an anthology because each of the seven studies was written at a different time with no deliberate connection to the other six. However, there is a thread running through these independent studies that ties them all together as they communicate different aspects of one unified message – being strategic in our spirituality. The first study deals directly with the interfaces discussed in the Bible where we connect with the world around us, the kingdom of heaven, and the kingdom of darkness. The second study in the series discusses finding the sensitive balance between two necessary interfaces – our need to spend time with God and our mandate to rise up and interact with the world. The third and fourth studies have to do with the biblical truths that we need to understand in order to accurately interface with our God, our world, and ourselves. In the letters to the seven churches of Asia Minor recorded in Revelation chapters two and there, only one of the churches is specifically mentioned as being at an interface; the church at Philadelphia is said to have an open door set before it. Interestingly, this is also the only church that is specifically mentioned as having a relationship with the Word of God. (Revelation 3:8, 10) The fifth study takes us through the life of one of our most beloved biblical heroes — David, the shepherd boy who killed a giant and wrote beautiful psalms. Although his life was riddled with one failure after another, he somehow attained the report that he was a man after God's own heart, which is the key to opening the doors of interface with the world that we learn about in the letter to the Philadelphian church. (Revelation 3:7) Next, we look at what it really means to have heart after the very heart of God – one that Bob Pierce, founder of World Vision, described as being broken with the same things that break the heart of God. Finally, the book concludes with a challenge to never fall short of the opportunities and blessing that God has provided for us as we interface with the One who sent us and those with whom we are to interface.

Israel – Key to Human Destiny

The Jewish people and the nation of Israel are puzzles and enigmas in world politics and human logic. How can it be that a group of people who account for less than one half of a percent of the world's population is responsible for one out of every five Nobel Peace prizes? Israel is so tiny a territory that no world map can even squeeze its name on the space allotted it on the layout, yet this minuscule nation dominates our evening news every night. Why is it that one little country of only a few million people can tie up the wealth, the foreign policy, and the political movements of the greatest nations on the face of the earth? Why is it that of all the ethnic groups in the world, only one bears the stigma (or honor) of having its name specifically coined into a word of hate and antagonism: anti-Semitism? The answers to these puzzling questions lie in the fact that these are no ordinary people and this is no ordinary piece of real estate. These are covenant people living in covenant land. Their destiny is charted by prophetic words from God Himself. Indeed, the saga of all mankind revolves around this people. Israel is the key to the human drama. Join Delron Shirley as he journeys into the past and glimpse into the future in order to understand the present.

The Last Enemy

Fear? Death? Defeated!! The Bible declares that death is our ultimate enemy and that the fear of death is a cruel warden that can hold us in the chains of slavery and bondage throughout our lives. BUT, our enemy Death has met his Waterloo and can no longer hold us in his power. In The Last Enemy, explore Passover weekend AD 33 changed your destiny.

Lessons Along the Way

Welcome to a journey that will lead you across the towering Himalayan Mountains, over rushing waterfalls, and into your own backyard. At each step of the journey and around each bend in the path, you will discover the most exciting thrills of life – not the rush of adrenalin released while crashing through the rapids of the Grand Canyon, not the spine-tingling chill of coming face-to-face with demonic supernatural forces, not the awesome hush of grandeur inspired by the majestic sunsets across the glacier polish of the majestic Sierra Nevada range – although all these and much more are included. You will discover the thrill of hearing the voice of God Himself speaking to you for direction and encouragement. Join us on this fascinating journey through life. Be ready to learn all the lessons along the way!

Living for the End Times

"The end is near!" "Jesus is coming back!" "These are the last days!" We all have heard these prophecies. Sometimes, we've heard them so often and over such a long period of time that they may have lost their impact. Yes, we believe that these are the last days, but we somehow keep living as if we think that things will always keep going as they always have and that nothing is ever going to change. Is it possible that we have given mental ascent to the concept of the end time but never let it really get hold of our lives? Let's explore what it means to live our lives as if we really believed that these are the end days – after all, they really are!

Maturing into the Full Stature of Jesus Christ

As a child, I learned a little song in children's church: "To be like Jesus, to be like Jesus. That's all I ask – just to be like Him." When I grew up, I realized that there was a whole lot more to becoming like Christ than just singing a little children's song. It has been said that going to church doesn't make you a Christian any more than sitting in the garage will make you an automobile or sitting in a donut shop will make you a policeman. There is a maturing process that we must go through if we ever hope to manifest the true nature of Christ in our lives. That maturing process demands that we have a total transformation in the way we think – that we be brainwashed, if you will. It requires more than just saying the right words; after all a parrot can speak English, but he is not an Englishman. In the same way, we must not settle for just learning the Christian jargon; we must be transformed into the very likeness of Christ through the renewing of our mentalities. You may not be what you think you are, but what you think – YOU ARE! Join Bible teacher Delron Shirley as he investigates how the way we think determines who and what we will be. Learn how your thinking can transform you into the full stature of Jesus Christ.

Maximum Impact

He showed up totally unannounced with no publicity agent, no campaign manager, and no budget to fund a campaign. Yet within three short weeks, he established a viable community of faith that was soon acknowledged and recognized as a role model throughout the world. Who was this man, and how did he flip the world one hundred eighty degrees on its axis? Join Bible teacher Dr. Delron Shirley as he makes a fascinating quest into the man, his methods, and the mission of a man who left maximum impact everywhere he went.

Of Kings and Prophets – Shapers of the Destinies of Nations

Bible teacher Dr. Delron Shirley invites you into his time machine to travel back through the corridors of time to visit the era of the Old Testament kings and prophets in the nations of Israel and Judah – the men who shaped the destinies of their nations. In walking through the encounters, interactions, and conflicts in the lives of these historical figures, we are constantly reminded of the words of the New Testament writer who said that everything that happened in the lives of these men serves as an example and a caution to us so we can make a difference in our own generation.

Passion for the Harvest – A Missions Handbook

We all know the Lord's statement that the harvest is plenteous but the laborers are few. However, I would like to suggest a little different consideration of the situation: the harvest is plenteous but the laborers are untrained. The cover photograph of a Nepali woman harvesting her grain not only pictures the primitive conditions in which the third world harvests their physical grain, it also helps us get a glimpse of the need for the entire Body of Christ to be trained for the spiritual harvest as well. In <u>Passion for the Harvest</u>, Bible teacher Delron Shirley exposes some of the pertinent truths necessary for preparing us for the challenge of the harvest. Learn how to sow in order to reap an abundant harvest and how to discern the harvest that the Lord is sending your way. Learn how to develop the resourcefulness and the expectant hope necessary to stand steadfastly until the harvest manifests and we discover new truths concerning the tools and the stamina necessary for reaping the full harvest. In short, develop a passion for the harvest!

People Who Make a Difference

Have you ever noticed that there are some people who just seem to stand out from the crowd? Although they may seem ordinary in so many ways, there is just some special something about them that identifies them as unique individuals. Though they may not be the "movers and shakers" that we think of as the ones who can push their way to the top of the corporate ladder, they somehow wind up leaving an indelible mark on their worlds. Let's explore what it is that makes some people the ones who make a difference. Better yet, let's learn how to be those individuals!

Positioned for Blessing and Power

In the first Psalm, David gave us a formula for a life that qualifies for God's blessings – be careful about where you walk, sit, and stand. In the book of Ephesians, the Apostle Paul gave us a formula on how to live in the power and authority of God – be determinate about where we sit, walk, and stand. In <u>Positioned for Blessing and Power</u>, Bible teacher Delron Shirley combines these two principles – one from the Old Testament and one form the New – in a way that can revolutionize your life.

Problem People of the Bible

In <u>Problem People of the Bible</u>, you will meet many of the biblical characters you have had to skip over as you did your daily reading because you simply couldn't understand exactly how their lives figure into the message of God's love and plan of salvation. This insightful story will help you make sense of their place in the grand scheme of the Bible and the story of God's dealings with the human family.

So, You Wanna Be A Preacher

A distillation of Delron Shirley's twenty-five years of mentoring young ministers and the evaluation of over ten thousand church services and sermons, <u>So You Wanna Be A Preacher</u> covers a wide range of topics from how to recognize and respond to the call into the ministry to tips on preparing and presenting your sermons and on getting them published. Special emphasis is given to helping you understand the minister's job description and recognizing how to manifest the Holy Spirit's presence in your ministry. The minister's personal life including discussion of ethics and etiquette is a major focus in the study. No matter what your ministry or calling, you are guaranteed to get new insights in your role as a minister and gain some helpful hints into effectively serving the Lord and His people.

Tread Marks

Does your life leave a mark on the people you meet and the circumstances you find yourself in? In Tread Marks, you'll learn a number of where-the-rubber-meets-the-road principles of successful Christian living that are guaranteed to ensure that you will leave a positive impression on individuals and society. Based on biblical principles and true life experiences, this book grapples with everyday life issues and presents simple but effective approaches to facing them successfully and victoriously. From the stories of the sinking of the Titanic and an African safari adventures to the expositions on Joshua's conquest of the Promised Land and Joseph's rise from slavery to the second most powerful man in Egypt, you'll be entertained, inspired, and motivated. You'll discover how your life can make a lasting impression.

A Verse for the Day (Two Issues are available)

In A Verse for the Day, Bible teacher Delron Shirley brings you a new insight into the Word of God each day with observations about the unique contributions the selected verses can make in our lives. Though the studies of these verses are by no means comprehensive or exhaustive, the fresh insights you'll gain in these daily visits with the Word of God are guaranteed to encourage, challenge, and inspire you in your walk with the Lord.

Women for the Harvest

"God's secret weapon" – that's how many people are coming to realize that we, as women are in the world of ministry. One example is, Dr. Yonggi Cho, who has the second largest church in the world. He has been quoted as saying, "Women are the greatest evangelistic tools. Someday the church will catch on." In this volume, author Peggy Shirley does an in-depth study into the history of why women have been forbidden from taking their God-given place in the church and explores the powerful biblical and historical examples of what happens when women are allowed to use the giftings which God has placed inside them. A revealing study of the scriptures which have long been used to block women from service, coupled with a motivational study on how to break free from the bondages which have held women back and a wealth of practical suggestions and advice -- this book is guaranteed to release you to become a true laborer in God's end-time harvest.

You'll be Darned to Heck if You Don't Believe in Gosh *and Other Musings*

This eclectic collection of mediations and musings addresses many issues concerning our Christian faith, including exactly what the Bible teaches about hell and who will go there, how prayer works, and how we should understand exactly who Jesus is. This study also takes you on a spiritual journey that delves into such topics as simple advice for Christian leaders and the biblical formula for radical change – both in your own personality and in the complexion of a whole nation.

Lighthearted at times, but always simple and straight forward, this refreshing study makes discovering theological truths from the scripture fun and enlightening. Buckle your seatbelt as you join Bible teacher Delron Shirley as he journeys to such interesting places as Nepal and Nigeria in quest of spiritual insight and revelation. You'll be glad that you came along for the adventure as you discover many simple truths that have always seemed just too difficult to understand.

Your Home Can Survive in the 21st Century

Have you ever heard someone say that we should get rid of old fashion ideas about marriage, family, and morals and add "After all, it is the twenty-first century"? With the rapid decline in traditional values, we might actually begin to question if our home will be able to survive in this new century. But there is good news if we only recognize that what is happening to the family today is a prophetic attack by the forces of the devil and that we are well equipped to fight back and conquer! Your home can not only survive – it can thrive!!

www.ingramcontent.com/pod-product-compliance
Lightning Source LLC
LaVergne TN
LVHW051201080426
835508LV00021B/2734